MyEasyJobSearch.com

F. Darnall Daley Jr.
&
F. D. "Dale" Daley III

ISBN: 1-4663-1230-0
ISBN-13: 9781466312302

Dedication

Dedicated to our wives, Ernie Daley and Kelly Daley, and in loving memory of our son and brother, Christopher Michael Daley, Sr.

Contents

Chapter 1
Introduction

In the days before the internet and email I'd hear people say, "I sent my resume to hundreds of companies and nobody has called me!" (BOOHOO!!) Today I hear people say, "I've emailed my resume to thousands of companies and nobody even emailed me back." (BOOHOO!!) Really! What did you expect? Did you think the process of emailing your resume to thousands of strangers would get you a job? Did you think that broadcasting your resume to the world would have people knocking on your door? Actually this method is successful just enough to keep the myth alive. But it's a low probability method. If this is all that you do, then you're in for a long, long period of disappointment and failure. In the pages that follow we hope we'll convince you of a better way.

So you've been fired! Or laid-off or down sized, or however you want to put it. Perhaps you're in a dead end job and need to escape. Fantastic! This may be the greatest opportunity of your life. Is that hard to believe? I'm sure that you find it impossible to believe that right now, especially if you are going through the pain of being out of work. The truth of the matter is that you just may wind up in a much better job, in a company that you really like better. In fact if you like the new job at all, it almost has to be better than the old one. It is most likely that you knew something was coming. That can't have been any fun. So being out of that situation has got to be a good thing in your life. During the early eighty's I went through a similar period when I had eight jobs in 54 months. During this period I was fired three times and failed in business once. This was a very exciting time in my life. I can understand just how exciting life is for you now, if you're going through the same kind of adventure.

On the other hand, perhaps you are a first time job seeker. You've just graduated from college or high school and you never had a serious job before. Well, I can understand just how exciting life is for you. Perhaps your parents are nagging you to get out and get a job. I'm sure you have some anxieties. This book is for you, too.

Not that I'm about to tell you that this is not a period of high stress. It is! Let me say that again, "IT IS!" It may be the most stressful time of your life. The point is that aside from the usual methods of reducing stress, you can minimize the stress by having a concrete plan for landing your next job. If you have a plan and you're following that plan, then you'll know that in due course you'll get the next job. It may take weeks or it may take months. But if you follow a good plan, then eventually you'll get a new job. That has got to make you feel better.

When I was doing my most extensive jobs-searching—in the early 1980's—things were different than now. I didn't really appreciate just how different until I recently read two books. The first was *The World is Flat* by Thomas Friedman. Friedman lists the 11 things that have flattened the world. The fact is that the world is smaller and flatter than it was in the 1980's. This is something that you'll have to take into account. The job that is available today may not be there tomorrow. Somebody who lives in some far away country may be doing that job. Or the economy may take a downturn that may eliminate the job. In fact that may be why you're interested in looking for a job right now. There was an article in the *Reading Eagle* recently about how to look for and find a job that won't be affected by the economy (*Reading Eagle*, June 4, 2008, quoting Erin Burt, *Kiplinger's Magazine*). The suggestion is that there are several areas that might be recession proof. These are: [1] Health Care—This is an area that will have continually growing demand as our population ages. [2] Education [3] Security—Crime doesn't stop in a recession. In fact it may very well increase. [4] Environmental Sciences—One would think that with all the crazy talk that goes on today about the environment this may be a growing area. [5] Government—Even though we would seem to have too much government already, the demand for government workers continues to grow; not just at the federal level but at all levels of government.

The second book was *Jobshift—How to Prosper in a Workplace Without Jobs* by William Bridges. While this book is not new, the idea is one that is becoming more and more important. Bridges' idea is that jobs are not just being exported, they are also disappearing. In the first place we are becoming more productive so we need fewer people to do the same amount of work. This of course doesn't help you find work. However, the second aspect may help. Jobs are disappearing because more and more business is being done by what have been called virtual companies. There is someone down the street from you sitting in their underwear in front of their computer running a multi-million dollar manufacturing company from their bedroom. They are doing the whole business over the computer. They have farmed out engineering, marketing, sales and accounting to others like themselves.

The manufacturing is done at some contract manufacturing facility far away. Order fulfillment is being done by a 4PL taking orders over the internet. This may be an opportunity for you but you won't find this opportunity in the usual places. If this is something that you think might be of interest, then you'll want to market yourself as a freelance worker and be alert for opportunities in this area. The beauty of this is that if you're doing a job for say six virtual companies and charging each one of them say one quarter of what you would normally expect to get in salary then that would be a very attractive situation for you.

I've talked with many, many people over the years who were out of work. Because of my own experience with unemployment, people have sought me out for advice on how to get a job. Usually people take a long time to get a new job because they don't have a plan to follow and because they don't work hard enough at getting work. Getting a new job is hard work. They send out a few resumes and then sit back and wait for someone to call them. Trust me. That won't work. If this is your plan, then you're in for a long wait.

What I need to tell you is no one ever calls. Your letters will not get answered. Your phone calls will not be returned. You will not hear that annoying ding as you receive an email offering that dream job. The good fairy is not going to call you with a job offer. It doesn't work that way. Well actually, it works that way just often enough to keep the myth alive. If you count on this method, however, you're very likely to be in for a great disappointment. You're also in for a long stretch of unemployment. Remember, whatever else is going on in the world, Murphy's Law has not been repealed.

If you want a new job, you're going to have to work at it. You're going to have to make phone calls, write letters, and do research. Yes, and you'll even have to send out some emails. You're going to have to get out and talk with people. It may be the hardest you've ever worked in your life. If you can't handle this, then you're in for a rough time. You'll just have to remain unemployed much longer than would otherwise be necessary.

In the chapters that follow we'll deal with all of the various aspects of how you should go about getting your next job. While we'll outline the methods, I want to make it quite clear that this is not a "cook book." No one can put the exact words in your mouth. The exact method has to be yours. I can tell you how to build the engine but you'll have to put in the gas and you'll have to steer the car. Most of all you'll have to put your foot on the accelerator. The harder you work, the sooner you find your new situation.

The bitter truth is that getting a job is about sales. If you've been in sales you'll immediately understand what I'm getting to. If you've not been inclined to take on sales jobs then you may be repelled by the thought. You've never been in sales and you don't want to be. Well, I'm as sorry as I can be about that. (NOT!) If you're looking for a job, then you're in sales. The good news is that there is a process to sales, that if you follow it, you'll make the sale. If you follow the process, you'll get the job you want. If you follow the process, getting your next job will be easy. It will be easy but it will be hard work.

The sales process is:

- Get to know the product. (That's you, Bunkie!)
- Find out who you suspect might be a customer for your product.
- Through research turn your suspects into prospects.
- Through presentation and closing make the sale.

In the pages that follow, we'll take you through this process.

Chapter 2
Some Points to Ponder

When my friend David Prine read my rough draft, he underlined some points that he thought were interesting. As you read along, you may notice these and find that they seem important to you too.

- If you're looking for a job, then you're in sales.
- You'll make a much better appearance if you are physically fit.
- Set up a daily schedule.
- The things that you are good at are the things that companies will pay you the most for doing.
- The culture or character of the company matters.
- The people least likely to have a positive influence whether or not you get a job in a particular company are the people in Human Resources or Personnel.

10

- Write down and practice what message you're going to leave.
- "Practice, practice, practice."
- "Are you ready to place an order now?"
- "Have I convinced you that I'm the person for this job?"
- The letter spells out point by point how your experience and qualification match the ones spelled out in the ad.
- http://www.MyEasyJobSearch.com.
- List your objective at the top of the resume.
- Do not burn any bridges.

Chapter 3
Dealing with Yourself

No matter why you're looking for a job, one of the most difficult people that you'll have to deal with during the process is yourself! You are the one who will decide how hard you will work at this. You are the one who decides if you'll learn by the inevitable failures that occur or if you'll be crushed by them. You are the one that will have to decide if you expect someone to hand you a job or if you understand that you'll have to bust your butt trying to find a new and better situation. You are the one who will have to keep your spirits up as you go through the process of finding your next situation.

❧❧

Dealing with Stress

Some of the most stressful events in your life are going to be (from most stressful to least stressful) death of spouse; divorce; marital separation; jail term; death of close family member (except spouse); major personal injury or illness; marriage; being fired from work; marital reconciliation; retirement. Other events that create stress in your life are business readjustment; change in financial state; change to different occupation; change in responsibilities at work; spouse begins or stops work; trouble with boss; change in work hours or conditions. If you are out of work or your situation is such that you have to look for work then you are experiencing one or more of these stressful life events. It is important that you recognize this and learn to deal with it. It could be one of the most stressful times in your life. Please note, however, that it isn't the stress but how you deal with it that harms you. If you are going to survive, you're going to have to learn to deal with this particular stress. Your first choice should be one of the non-destructive methods for dealing with stress. The destructive methods of dealing with stress such as drink, drugs, gambling and suicide are not good solutions. I mention this because these are just the things that may occur to you.

Furthermore, you need to deal with the stress because there is no way you're going to land a new position with your voice quaking with fear or your eyes half closed from lack of sleep. That paralyzing feeling of desperation that comes over you will not help you reach a happy solution to your situation. So you must find a way to deal with this.

Some of the areas that others have explored to reduce stress are:

a.   Religion—If you are a religious person and perhaps belong to a religious congregation this may help you reach a peace of mind. Furthermore, the members of the church that you belong to may be part of your support group. If you belong to a church, this is not the time to neglect either your membership or your religious duties.

b.   Exercise—This is especially important. Get a good exercise program going, if this has not been your regular habit. Continue your program, if you have been on a regular program. Don't drop your membership at the gym to save money. You need exercise more than ever now. If you have not been exercising regularly, start. If you've gotten out of shape as the years have rolled by, now is the time to correct the situation. You'll make a much better appearance if you are physically fit.

14

c. Meditation—I didn't really understand this until a recent speaker at
a Rotary meeting showed us how to
meditate. This can be very relaxing.

d. Other activities such as hobbies—
Note, however, that this may not be
a good time to spend lavishly on a
hobby. If you really enjoy a particular
hobby, you may want to think about
turning this into a business.

e. Community service work—There are
two sides to this. On the one hand
you don't want to get carried away
with this. Don't spend so much time
that you interfere with the main job of
changing your situation. On the other
hand, you will meet people who can
either support you or help you find a
new situation.

f. Working very hard at getting the next
job—This method must be used with
care. It is important to work very, very
hard at finding the next opportunity.
However, the old cliché, "All work
and no play, makes Jack a dull boy,"
works overtime when you're under
stress. Balance is the key. Getting a
new job is a business that you will like-

ly do out of your home. Unless you set limits this can get out of hand. When the office is just down the hall, it's all too easy to work all kinds of hours.

෩෨

Dealing with Resentment and Bitterness

One of the first questions that you'll ask after you've been fired or laid-off is, "Why me?" "Why should I be the one?" "What did I do to deserve this?" Next comes the bitterness and resentment towards your former employers. This is natural, but you cannot afford to indulge in this type of thinking for long. You have to put this behind you. I believe that it's healthy to spend a few minutes every day plotting revenge against the near sighted, unscrupulous, roguish, low intelligence, knuckle dragging individuals and the companies that appreciated your worth and talents so little that they actually had the nerve to fire you. This is natural and healthy as long as you don't become obsessive about it. A few minutes of harmless plotting are O.K. If it becomes more than this, for example, if you start to make notes, or if you start reading the ads in the back of supermarket magazines with an eye to start hiring mercenaries, then you have gone too far. You have a major problem that has to be dealt with. Seriously! Seek professional help of the kind that seems most appropriate to your circumstances.

Thus, while bitterness is natural, you have to get over it. Furthermore, you must never, never, never, ever let any of this bitterness and resentment show in any of your discussions with a prospective employer. And everybody you talk with is a prospective employer. So put the bitterness and revenge out of your mind. Bitterness is a drink that someone else can pour for you, but for it to have any effect on you, you have to lift the cup to your lips and you have to swallow. Remember, the best revenge is to get a job with the competitor and do such a fantastic job that you put your former company out of business. Cool! Think about that for a minute! That's sweet revenge!

If you feel that the circumstances that put you in a position to have to look for a job are unfair, it's OK to get mad and throw things. This is natural. Express your anger. But get over it. Get over yourself. Move on. Don't dwell on how unfair the world is. The world is unfair. Get over it. Move on.

శ్ర-శ్ర

Setting Goals

Throughout this book we will talk about setting goals. People who set goals achieve far more than those who don't. The overriding goal is to get a job. Not only is this overriding but it can be overwhelming as well. As you go through your job campaign, set goals for yourself. Set daily goals. For example, today I'm going to research three prospects and make calls to set up at least two interviews. Set up a daily schedule. Start work at a regular time. If you're working out of your home, dress for work. Don't sit around in your "pj's." If you let yourself develop sloppy habits, you'll not make the best use of your time.

But don't overdo it. Not only should you have a regular start time but you should have a regular quit time. When you are working out of your home, it is easy to find yourself working all the time. There will be days when you have to work long hours. However, if you don't set some limits, you'll kill yourself before you ever get a job.

෨ඏ

Keeping Your Spirits Up

Keep your spirits up. When you are working, you get rewarding social interactions from the people that you work with every day. When you have lost your job, you no longer have this available to you. It is very easy at this stage to loose sight of your self-worth. Look yourself in the mirror and tell yourself that you're really terrific. Do this regularly; it'll do wonders for your spirits. When I was in the throes of job searching, I used to start each day by looking is the mirror and saying, "I'm nine feet tall and I can walk through brick walls." I had this written on a 3x5 card that I kept in my pocket. The other side read, "It was not my fault." Sound silly? Well, maybe. But it worked for me and it may very well work for you. Try it sometime.

Chapter 4
The "Whats"

There are two questions that you'll have to answer in the process of finding your next situation. These are: "What do you bring to the party?" and "What do you want to do?" Answering these two questions will help you with the first step in the sales process—"Get to know the product."

☙❧

"What do you bring to the party?"

If you owned the company, would you hire yourself? If you own the company, the only reason to hire anybody is so that you can make a profit. So the question you have to be prepared to answer is, "If I owned this company, how could hiring me make me more profit?" thus the question, "What do I bring to the party?" Or stated another way, "Why would someone want to hire me?"

☙❧

"What do you want to do?"

The next task is to decide what you want to do. Most people start the job search process by working on their resume. This may be therapeutic but it doesn't move you toward your goal of getting a job. The simple fact is that you may not want another job. You may want to start a new business. You may want to become a freelancer.

Do you really want a new job or another job? Many people take the fact of being fired and turn it into the opportunity to start their own company or business. If this is the route that you want to take, you should, by all means investigate it. You should understand though that starting and owning your own business is risky. Most new companies fail. You may not be one of those people that are constitutionally able to stand being on their own. The chances are that, if this is what you really wanted to do, you would have already done it. Nevertheless, this chapter is about reviewing your options and, if owning your own business is one of your options, then by all means have a really good look at it.

Another alternative to full time employment is to take temporary assignments. There are staffing firms that will help you find these assignments. The way it works is companies contract with the employment agency to send them temporary workers. The agency hires the workers and takes care of paying them. The company pays the agency a premium over the wage paid by the agency. Of course, the pay scale will vary depending on the particular position. If the company decides to hire you permanently, changing your status from temporary to permanent, the agency is paid a fee, usually on a sliding scale depending on how long you were working as a "temp." Usually, after a specified period of time, the fee is waived. Many companies will clarify up front if a position is just temporary vs. temp-to-hire/temporary-to-permanent. Many companies use temporary workers as a part of their workforce. This allows workers to get their foot in the door of a great company and gives them a chance to prove themselves. You get to take a good look at them and they get to take a good look at you. Some start all employees as "temps." Nor is temporary work confined to just clerical or factory workers. Temporary employment covers a wide variety of skills and professions from accounting to medicine to engineering. I have met a number of people who based their whole career on temporary assignments.

So in answering the question, "What do you want to do?" some of your alternatives are:

- Full time job
- Temporary assignments
- Temporary to permanent job
- Work freelance
- Start a business

ॐॐ

Gathering the Data

So we have two questions: "What do you bring to the party?" and "What do you want to do?" In order to answer these two questions you need to take an inventory of your skills and desires. You need to have a plan for what you want to do with the rest of your life. How can you find a job, if you don't know what kind of job you want? How much time will you waste looking for a job if what you really want is to start a business? If you don't take this first step, you may wind up in the same kind of situation that you just left.

The next thing to think about is what you are good at. Companies hire people because what they can do is a good investment for the company. Stop and think about that for a moment. The work that you do adds value to the company. The reality is that there are no unimportant jobs in any company. Every job is there because the work that the people doing the job make money for the company. This is what it's all about. If the company doesn't make money from your work, then it should not have you on the payroll. If you are not making money for your company, the time will come when they discover this and you'll be fired. If you don't understand this, then you need to brush up on the fundamentals of economics. A fuller discussion of the theory of economics is beyond the scope of this book. The point is that you need to discover (and be able to articulate) what you are good at. You need to be able to tell prospective employers how they are going to profit from having you on the payroll. If you can't do this, then you have to ask yourself why anybody would hire you. The things that you are good at are the things that companies will pay you the most for doing.

The same applies if you are planning to start a business of your own. What are you good at? If you are going to be in business, you need to base that business on your skill set. It needs to be about something that you're good at or you will fail.

Another way to ask the same question is to ask, "What are you experienced at doing?" The things that you have experience at doing are the things that you have special knowledge about. These are the special skills that you bring to a new job. There is no substitute for having experience. Of course, nobody can really appreciate the value of experience until you have it.

The next item to think about is what are the things that you enjoy doing. All other things being equal, you'll be better rewarded for doing things that you enjoy doing than for doing things you don't enjoy. This is because you bring a better attitude to the tasks that bring you joy.

In the end you have to decide what you want to do. It may have been Yogi Berra who said, "If you don't know where you're going, when you get there you may find that you're somewhere else." Think about that a minute and you'll see how that applies to your situation. You need a direction. You need a plan. You need to focus your efforts. If you don't have direction, you'll run around in circles until you drop from exhaustion. Having a plan, on the other hand, will not contribute to your stress level.

It is certainly possible that you'll wind up with a job that you don't like, in a company that you hate, working with people that you don't like. Economic necessity may drive you to this. But before that happens, you need to do everything that you can to give yourself an opportunity to find a job that you like, in a company that you believe in, working with people that you really enjoy. To do that you need to develop a job campaign that focuses in on the things you like to do and on the things that you're good at.

As the following paragraphs unfold you'll find that I'm a great believer in making lists. So let's start this task by making some lists. In compiling your list, write them for yourself. You can edit them for public viewing later. This is about you getting a better understanding of you. It is the first step in the sales process of getting to know the product.

The first list is of your accomplishments. Write a short paragraph about each episode in your career that you're especially proud of. Be specific. Use numbers. "Reduced inventory 27% in two years." is much more impressive than, "Worked very hard at reducing inventory," or "Was responsible for inventory reduction." "Completed six projects on time and on budget" is much better than "Was Project Manager."

The second list is of the times that you had fun. Again write a short paragraph about the times that you enjoyed yourself the most. Hopefully, some of these times will be work related.

The second best hope is that, if these times of joy don't relate to work, then they will suggest inquiries into new avenues of endeavor. For example, if your most enjoyable moments have been mountain climbing, them maybe your next job needs to be as a mountain guide. That is, the list of enjoyable times may suggest some other lines of work that you might enjoy more than those you engaged in in the past.

Next list the things about the companies that you've worked for that you liked. Companies have character. There is a culture in every company. Were you asked or forced to do things that went against your value system? Did you like the way you and your fellow workers were treated? Did you dislike the way customers were treated? Was concern for safety emphasized? Was it a small company or a large one? What was the management style like? These are elements of the culture and character of a company. What was the culture like in the companies that you've worked in that you liked? What was the culture like in these companies that you didn't like? I have worked in a number of companies when there was an ownership or management change. This usually changed the culture of the company. It was interesting to watch as some people became uncomfortable with the new culture. It was interesting to observe my own feelings about this. The culture or character of the company matters. This will help you decide on the type of company that you'd like to work for. Finally, list the things that you didn't like about companies that you have worked for. This will give you a warning about things to look out for in companies that you talk to.

Finally, make a list of your skill set. What are the things that you do well? What does your experience suggest that you do really well? What training courses have you taken? What did these courses prepare you to do? What advanced education have you had? Don't neglect to list skills that you've developed as a result of your hobbies. What skills have you learned during your volunteer activities?

&~&

Making a Decision

Examine all of these lists and see if they suggest to you what it is that you want to do. Are you beginning to see a pattern emerging? Does this help you decide about the kind of job you want to look for? Do these lists help you visualize the kind of company you want to work for?

Another use for these lists is that they will help you develop the presentations that you want to make to your prospects, the potential employers, that you will meet and interview. Thus you need to keep going over these lists and revising them. The more times that you review and revise your lists the more likely it is that you will cover all of the ground that needs to be covered. Write and revise! Write and revise!

In summary then, you need to decide what you bring to the party and what you want to do.

I. Make a list of your accomplishments.

II. Make a list of the things you've done that you enjoyed or were fun.

III. Make a list of the things you like about companies that you've worked for.

IV. Make a list of the things you didn't like at companies that you've worked for.

V. Make a list of your skill set.

VI. Revise the paragraphs that you've written.

VII. For good measure, revise again.

VIII. Decide what you want to do!

IX. Learn to articulate what you bring to the party.

These last two may be the hardest. Perhaps you will come up with a few options. It's not necessary to make a hard and fast decision. It will, however, be necessary to have a small list of options. You need to know where you're headed. As we noted before, it may have been Yogi Berra who said, "If you don't know where you're going, when you get there you may find that you're somewhere else."

In fact you may not need to make a decision but just keep your options open. As you talk with potential employers, be alert for opportunities to work freelance or as a consultant. The same interview could cover all three. In my checkered career I've had what I thought was a job interview turn into a consulting assignment. I've also been hired full time by consulting clients. I remember one potential employer/client who said to me, "Mr. Daley, I'm confused. Are you here looking for a job or are you trying to sell me consulting services?" Of course, I had to tell him that I was. He had caught me. I was keeping my options open. I was in his office selling consulting services but I would have been open to a discussion of a job offer. Keep your options open.

Chapter 5
How to get a Job

I think that we can assume at this point that you've decided that you want another job. Why else would you be still reading a book on how to get a job? You now have an idea about the kind of work you want to do. You have a picture of the kind of job you want and the kind of company you want to work in. Or perhaps your picture at this point is not all that focused. You will at least have taken a good look at the alternatives. As time goes on it will get clearer.

Suspects

The next step is to establish a list of all of the companies that you **suspect** that you might want to work for. Don't be in the least bit critical at this stage. If the company exists and you suspect, even slightly, that you might want to work for it, include it on your list. At this point whether or not the company has any job openings is not part of the equation. It is totally irrelevant.

All companies have openings at some point. Whether they do now is not important.

You can find out about companies from a variety of sources. First of all you have your own knowledge. Write down the names of companies that you know about. Don't forget to include former employers. They may now realize the error of their ways in letting you get away. Talk with your friends. Go to the library and look at the reference material on firms in your area. When I was involved with this activity in the 80's this was the only option. Today the easiest way is to go on-line and look at the websites of the companies in your area. Don't forget news reports. The business section of your local newspaper will often have articles about local companies.

You should start with a list of about fifty names. If you can't come up with fifty immediately, don't be concerned about it. You'll discover more company names later. If you come up with more, that's great; the more the merrier. As you go on, you'll be reviewing and revising this list. Review and revise, which may sound familiar from the last chapter. Just remember that you're the one in charge of your job search. You decide what to put on the lists, not someone else.

ॐॐ

Prospects

The second step is to do research on your suspects and turn them into **prospects**. You do this by finding out everything that you can about the company in question. There is a danger here that you'll spend an inordinate amount of time doing research on a company that is not a good prospect. The way to avoid doing this is to look initially for reasons to eliminate a company from your list. If you know, for example, that you would never want to work for a particular company, cross them off of the list immediately. Don't waste time on it. If you read in the paper that the company in question has just had a massive layoff, cross them off your list. Unless you have very special skills, the chances of you landing a job with that firm are very slim. Cross them off. Don't be shy about this elimination process. We're talking here about preserving your most precious commodity, your time. And if circumstances change, you can always put them back on the list.

Your research needs to be aimed at two things. One, you need to decide if this is a company that you'd like to work for. How do you decide this? I don't know, you tell me. You're the one looking for a job. Perhaps you like the products or services that the company provides. Perhaps you like what you discover about the work environment in a particular company. Review the list that you prepared earlier on what you liked at companies that you worked for. Look at the list of things you didn't like at companies that you've worked for. The purpose of these lists was to help you answer this question. Companies have character just as people do. You want to find a company whose character or personality is compatible with yours. Perhaps you have a number of friends working at the company who say they enjoy their work life. Other questions that you might ask because these things are important to you are:

Is the company growing? Growing companies will more than likely provide the most opportunity in the future. In other words, how many times in your life do you want to go through this job search routine? If you want to minimize the number of times, then you want to find a growing company.

Is the company small? Are you looking for a small company?

Is the company large? Are you looking for a large company? Do you feel more at home in a large company?

Is the company close to you? Do you want to stay in your present location? Is the company farther away? Do you want to relocate? Is it near your family? Do you want to move back home?

And so on. You get the idea. All of this is aimed at deciding if this is the company for you.

Doing research on companies is much easier than it used to be. In the good old days we had to go to the library and look up public information on companies. You had to call the company or a stock broker to get an annual report. Today much of the information you need in on-line. Can you say, "Google?" Most companies today have their own websites. You can download the annual report in a .PDF file from their website. You can find SEC filings online.

The second focus of your research is to discover the names of the people that you might work for, if you worked in that company. Who is the man or the woman who would be your boss? Who is their boss? Who manages the other functions in other departments? Who is the number two? The reason for wanting this bit of information is that this is the person who will decide if you get a job at the company. There will be other people at your chosen company who will influence this decision. You need to find out, if you can, who these people are, too. Research these people too. Again, can you say, "Google"?

The people least likely to have a positive influence whether or not you get a job in a particular company are the people in Human Resources or Personnel or whatever they're calling themselves these days. Their job is to keep you out of the company. The last people you want to be talking to in a company are the people in this department. We'll get into this more when we talk about answering ads in the newspaper. For now, let's just say that there are exceptions, but for the most part, they're the last people in a company or an organization to find out about an opening. Therefore, they're the last people you want to be in touch with.

Your sources for your research are:

- Newspapers, current issue.
- Company websites
- On-line research
- Newspapers, back issues. Check the library. Check on-line.
- Catalogs of company products
- Annual and quarterly reports of public companies.

- SEC filings
- Friends, especially those working for the organization in question.
- Acquaintances, especially those working for the organization in question.
- People you meet casually, especially those working for the organization in question. Remember every conversation is a potential job interview.
- Professional Societies—Do you belong to an appropriate professional society? If not, you should join. It will be good for networking.
- Libraries
- Chamber of Commerce—The Chamber of Commerce for your area will probably have a website where you will find listings of the names of companies and of the names some of their key personnel.

Use all of these resources to research the companies on your suspect list to turn the suspects in to prospects by deciding:

Is this a company you would want to work for?

If you did work for this company, whom would you work for?

The next question, of course, is how to get a job at one of these companies.

ॐॐ

The Job Campaign

Up to this point we've talked about what you want to do. We've made lists of the possible companies that you might work for. And we've done research on these organizations to see if these suspects are really prospects that might someday be your company. Those of you that have been in sales may recognize the process that we've been going through so far as a familiar one. Everyone in sales goes through the task of identifying prospects. Those of you that have never been in sales, I'm about to let you in on a secret. Pay attention to this because it is important. If you've never had a sales position in your life, you have one now. Not only do you have a sales position but you're also the Sales Manager. The product that you're selling is yourself. You have got to convince someone that you are worth more than the exorbitant salary that you're asking for your services. As we have outlined above the sales process is a simple one.

- Get to know the product.

- Find out who you suspect might be a customer for your product.
    o Identify potential customers
    o Make a list of these suspects
- Through research turn your suspects into prospects.
- Through presentation and closing make the sale.
    o Develop a sales presentation
    o Find a way to get face to face with your prospect
    o Make the sales presentation
    o Close the sale

What we need to talk about at this point is how to map out this campaign. What are you going to say when you get face to face with your future boss and she says, "Well, what did you want to see me about?"

Go back to your list of accomplishments. Prepare a written short speech about each of those accomplishments. Practice those speeches. Give the speech to a friendly audience before taking it on the road. After you give a speech to a prospective employer, review how it went and decide if you want to revise it. Review and revise; that may sound familiar from an earlier chapter.

Also remember that sales is a numbers game. The whole idea is to get to a "Yes" from a prospect. But some of your prospective customers will say "No." Is that exciting or what? You have to learn to take the "No's" in stride. One of the ways to do this by playing the numbers game. If the odds are 10:1 against you getting a job offer from a prospect and you want ten job offers then you have to make a solid pitch to 100 prospects. In trying to get a job you really don't know what the odds are. The reality is that not everyone you talk to is going to offer you a job. So you need a number of prospects. Also remember that you're going to hear a lot of "No's." Those "No's" will come in many forms. For example, "We're not hiring," "We don't have any openings," or "You'll have to check with Human Resources."

Also you don't know what hidden criteria might exist. I had a very good friend that had a long very successful career. Over the years he hired many people. But he had a strange quirk that I could never get him to explain. He would watch to see how a prospective employee parked their car. If they backed the car into the parking place, he wouldn't hire them. If you were going for that interview, how would you know about that? It may even be that the people you're talking to don't even know themselves about these hidden criteria. Maybe it's because you part your hair on the left. Or laugh too much or don't laugh enough. You have no way of knowing. All of these things are out of your control. So don't worry that you get turned down. Keep on working your plan and have plenty of prospects on your list.

৯৹৽

Setting Up Interviews

The way to get job interviews is to call and make an appointment. This is the way that you'd do it if you had a product to sell. However, if you call someone and ask if they have any job openings, they'll either tell you no, or they'll tell you to contact the Human Resources Department. At this point you don't need to know if there is a job opening. Your objective is to get yourself face to face with a person who might likely be your boss someday. In this way you'll find out what your future boss needs. If you're the answer to those needs, your future boss will create a job for you. Keep this in mind when we later talk about answering ads from newspapers or on-line. The job you are eventually offered may not even exist at the time of your first interview.

This is such a strange idea that I'll try to explain it in another way. Some studies have shown that a high percentage of jobs that people get were not planned when the prospective employer first met the job hunter.

How can this be? Well, every manager at every level in every business has problems; problems that they are trying to solve. Many of these problems walk around on two feet. They have these problems in mind when they meet someone. The thought process thus evolves. If this person worked for me, the "such-and-such" problem might be solved. Put another way, if we give this person a job, we'll make more profit because they will solve the "such-and-such" problem.

So what do you say? Well, this is your job search, so you'll have to decide this. You might think about approaches such as:

*I need to visit you to get advice about my career.

*Want to find out whom I should see in the community.

*I need advice on how to proceed.

*I'm doing research on your company to see if it is a company I'd like to work for.

Everybody in your situation is reading books about how to get a job. All of them will give you advice on what to say to get to see someone or what to say in a letter. If you follow this advice, word for word, you'll sound exactly like all of the others. What you need to come up with is something that is uniquely yours. Be honest. An outrageous lie may get you by the secretary but it's not likely to get you a job. At the same time remember that it is not necessary to tell everything that you know.

If you have never been in sales and are not used to this process, you'll need to practice calling people and setting up appointments. The idea is to reveal just enough to get the appointment. If you say too much and get turned down over the phone, you won't have achieved your objective of getting face to face with your future boss. Many people have told me that they did best when they started with friends and acquaintances. Call up some of your friends and make appointments to see them. Try out your sales presentation on them. After you have done a number of these you'll feel a lot more comfortable with the process. Then you'll be ready to try it out on strangers.

If you're a young person, one approach that seems to have success is to ask for an appointment to get advice one how to pursue your career goals. Likewise, if you're older or a more mature person, you could ask for advice on what direction your career could take now.

෬৵৵

Telephone Skills

When I call someone on the phone I sometimes ask, "Have I caught you at a good time?" Any answer to this question but, "No", is a, "Yes." If a person says, "No," then you should ask when you could call back. The best way to do this is to say, "Would you prefer that I call back this afternoon, or would tomorrow morning be better for you?" In this way you have made an appointment to have a telephone conversation. Any other response but a "No" means "Yes." If the person you've called gives you a, "Yes" then they have agreed to hear what you have to say rather than think about what they can do to get you off of the phone so that they can get back to work. This doesn't mean that you now have all day. It means that you have about 30 seconds to state your case. Make the most of that time.

Sometimes you won't get through to the person that you're calling. Did I say sometimes? Does anybody actually answer their damn phone anymore? Write down and practice what message you're going to leave. Even though it seems that people never call back, they sometimes actually do. Therefore, you have to have an answering machine. If they can't leave a message for you, they may call the next person on their list. It happens. I personally know of cases where people who sent resumes in answer to ads didn't get an interview because they couldn't be reached.

Prepping For an Interview

Once scheduled for an interview, it is time to prepare yourself. An interview is like any competitive situation. The way to land the position is to perform better then your competition (the other applicants).

- Learn what you can about the company. The internet can be a great source of information.
- If you know the name of anyone who is going to interview you, research them. It is amazing the amount of information that is available on individuals. You do not want to go into an interview with someone who has a 10 page Wikipedia write-up and you didn't know about it. The same thing

applies to the officers of the company. You need to know as much as you can learn. Knowledge is power.

- Dress professionally
- Plan what positive aspects about yourself you wish to come out during the interview. Study these repeatedly in the days before your interview. Planning ahead and practicing will help you remember these attributes even if you become nervous during your interview. Prepare answers to common questions such as, "Why did you leave your last position" or "Tell me about yourself". Always present your answers in a positive fashion. NEVER speak poorly or negatively about a previous employer. People will feel that if you're negative about your previous employer, you'll be negative about them. Besides, except for me, nobody cares about your tale of woe. And actually I don't care all that much either. Get it?
- Sometimes you will be informed on what type of Interview you can expect. (See Types of Interviews) If you were not informed it would be best to be ready for any of the types.
- Prepare one or two questions to ask at the end of the interview. Information

about the company or the benefits it offers are good subjects however it is not wise to ask questions like, "What are the company's leave benefits."

o What are the opportunities for advancement and do you typically promote from within?

o What types of training programs do you offer?

o While researching your firm I learned (fill in the blank). Can you tell me more about that?

o Can you tell me what my average day might be like?

o What happened to the person who previously held this role?

• Plan on arriving at least 30 minutes in advance to ensure that you are on time. In the Boy Scouts we say, "To be early is to be on time. To be on time is to be late. To be late is unthinkable." This is a good rule for going on an interview. If you arrive early, this will give you time to become comfortable with the surroundings and forget about the traffic you just had to fight.

• Park your car in a visitors spot. Many companies will watch to see where you parked. And then there was the guy who threw his beer can in the trash can outside the company entrance. Wasn't that considerate of him?

- Wear business formal attire for the area where you live. If that means a suit, wear a suit. If the prospective employer tells you not to wear a suit, then wear business casual clothes. Always err on the side of being dressed professionally.
- Bring a "cheat sheet" with you. If you have to fill out an application, you'll need the names and addresses of former employers.
- Bring extra copies of your resume. You never know how many people you'll meet and talk to. Also it helps to have a supply of calling cards that list your contact information.

છ•જ

Types of Interviews

Traditional

This is your basic interview consisting of one or more interviewers and yourself. You can expect questions about your work history, qualifications, your impression of your former company or former boss (remember, remain positive), how many days you usually miss work in a year, *etc.*

Behavior Based

An interviewer in a behavioral based interview is looking for you to share with them times in your past when your actions satisfied the requirements of the question. These questions could sound like, "Tell us about a time when you had difficulty meeting a deadline" or "Tell us about a time when you helped your company become more profitable." Remember, the interviewer will not be interested in your philosophy on how to solve a problem; they will be looking for you to give an example of a time when you were able to put your philosophy into action. They're looking for you to give a narrative that demonstrates your actions. However, this is not the time to tell negative stories about yourself. Be prepared to tell positive stories.

Situational

These interviews are set up in a fashion where you are given a hypothetical problem and told what resources you have at your disposal to satisfactorily resolve the situation. Upon completion of the project the applicant then can meet with interviewers to share their resolution as well as answer additional interview questions. I know of one company where they sit you down at a computer and ask you to solve a simulated problem.

Panel

When more then one interviewer sits in on the interview, this is considered a panel interview. Generally there are preset questions that the interviewers ask in a round robin fashion and make notes on your responses.

Others

Companies are trying to see if you fit with them. They also want to see how you react. I remember one interview just before I graduated from college. The interviewer asked me the solution to a particular engineering problem. I told him I didn't know the answer but briefly outlined my approach to solving the problem. He then confessed he didn't know the answer either. We then spent 30 minutes working on the problem. I got a job offer from this company and ultimately went to work for them.

At another interview the room was dark with only a small light on the interviewer's desk that almost cast light on his face. There were other people in the room that were not introduced but who asked me questions. I told the human resources representative who came to get me after the interview not to bother to call me for a second interview. As desperate as I was for work at that point, I wasn't going to go to work for that company.

෯෯

First Impressions

Be advised, you are being evaluated the moment you walk into a company's lobby. It is the individual's job, who handed you the application, to prescreen all applicants to ensure they meet the position's basic requirements, have suitable availability and present themselves in a professional manner. If you do not make a good first impression with this individual, your chances of landing the position of your interest will be slim to none. These individuals can be good sources of information about the position and the company. The trick is to try and time your visit to the lobby when it is not very busy so you can get their undivided attention. You might find this window of time to be in the afternoon, but allow yourself enough time to complete the application process before they close for the day.

Most companies now allow you to apply for positions on-line. In this case the prescreening process involves what are called "Knock out Questions". These are basic questions about your qualifications, availability and other critical requirements of the position.

Most companies will call back applicants, to schedule interviews, after they have had a chance to review the applications. Employers with a large number of openings have been known to conduct on the spot interviews. It is important to go with the flow of the particular employer with whom you have applied. Asserting yourself by demanding an interview will not serve your cause well.

෮෧

Controlling the Interview

Develop a sales presentation. What are you going to say? Write it down. Rehearse. Remember the old story about the man who asked a New Yorker how to get to Carnegie Hall. The answer was, "Practice, practice, practice." Well, this applies to you now. Practice what you're going to say. Practice it aloud. Practice it aloud in front of a mirror. Practice in front of your spouse. If you want a really tough audience, make your kids sit and listen. Especially if they're teenagers and think they know everything. Practice! Practice! Practice!

෮෧

Interview Questions

There are a number of interview questions that for some reason people like to ask. Not only to get information from you but also to see how you handle yourself. The trick is to be prepared with answers that help your cause, not to stumble through answering a question and sink your ship in the process. Some of these questions are:

"Where do you want to be five years from now?"

"What are your major strengths?"

"What are you most proud of in your work history?"

"What do some co-workers do that annoys you?"

"Which of your job skills do you think need improving?"

"What are you least proud of in your work history?"

"What did you like most about the last place you worked?"

"Who was your favorite boss?" "Why?"

"What kinds of situations get you in trouble at work?"

"What did you like least about the last place you worked?" Be really careful when you answer this one. Remember, nobody likes a complainer.

"What are your major weaknesses?" Try to turn this into something positive.

"What was your greatest accomplishment?"

"Why did you leave your last job?" Be sure you have a well rehearsed story line for this one, especially if the circumstances were not benign. Full disclosure is not necessary but honesty is.

"What was your worst mistake?" Again try to turn this into something positive.

You will hear many more questions like these. Everybody who conducts interviews has their favorites. Because you have prepared answers to some questions, you'll be better able to answer questions that you haven't heard before. Remember with these kinds of questions, you don't really have to answer the question that is asked, you only have to appear to. For example, in the case of the last question you might answer the question, "What mistake did you make that taught you the most interesting lesson?" Whatever you do don't actually tell about your <u>worst mistake</u>. Unless it was so bad that it was published in the newspaper, there is no way your prospective employer can know. Because of your preparation you have developed little stories about yourself that present you in a positive light. Think of how politicos answer questions, when they're running for office. Whatever the question is, they turn very quickly to their prepared campaign speeches and you should, too.

Furthermore, there are things about the company that they're not going to tell you about either. There is a picture that hangs in my office. It shows a cowboy. Under the picture is a caption that reads, "Thar were things about this outfit they didn't tell me afor I signed on." This is always the case. Full disclosure is never the practice nor is it desirable in an employment interview. And don't take this as an opportunity to say something negative about your old employer. No matter how bad they were; no matter how much dirt they did you, keep your mouth shut on that score and get on with your life. And unbelievable as it might

seem, your prospective employer isn't interested in your sad tale. Do you want sympa-
thy or do you want a job? Nobody wants to
hire someone who might later badmouth him
or her. Nobody wants somebody around who
sounds bitter and resentful.

Write out answers to these questions and
memorize the answers. Practice giving the
response so that you seem natural giving it.
When you are asked a question that you've
not heard before, add it to your list of questions
and develop an answer. Also, as mentioned
above, when you're asked a question that you
haven't heard before, do what the politicians
do—answer a question that you do have an
answer for.

ॐॐ

Closing

When we train new sales people, the hardest point to get across is getting them to ask
for the order. They go through a sales presentation, say goodbye, and walk out of the potential customer's office without asking for an
order. When we ask them why they didn't get
an order they tell us that the customer wasn't
ready to buy. How did they know? They didn't
ask. You must end every sales presentation with

some variation of, "Are you ready to place an order now?" When you do this you get feedback on how your presentation was received by the potential customer. Whatever your potential customer says in answer to your carefully worded question other than, "I'm never going to buy anything from you," is a potential, "Yes." And getting to, "Yes," is the whole point of every sales situation.

Translating this into the language of the job search means that at the close of an interview you have to ask, "Have I convinced you that I'm the person for this job?" or "When can I start?" You may not like the answer that you get at this point. You may be told, "No!" But if you don't ask, you'll spend the next three weeks expecting a phone call that's never going to come. At the same time you may be told something that will give you an opportunity to rescue the situation. For example, you may be told that your last salary was more than they're prepared to pay in the new job. This will give you a chance to explain that you don't consider that a problem. You may be told that your experience doesn't match what they're looking for. This will give you an opportunity to give a more detailed explanation of your relevant experience. The point is that if you don't ask, you'll never know.

58

I understand that this is difficult to do. When you ask a closing question, you invite rejection. But by asking where you stand, you get information that you need to land a job. If it doesn't work with this potential employer, it will help you refine your presentation skills.

Prepare and practice some closing questions for different situations. In that way you'll be prepared to use them at the end of the interview. Remember...ask for the order.

❧❦

Follow Up

No matter what the outcome of an interview, you must follow up. A letter will do very nicely for this. And remember that every meeting is an interview. Enclose a copy of your resume with your letter. This will help remind them who you are. You can't believe how helpful this is to people conducting a number of interviews.

Go back to someone who hired someone else after about three months. It may be that the first person didn't work out. It may be that there is another opening.

❧❦

Answering Newspaper Ads

Go ahead and answer ads in the newspaper. Some people actually get jobs this way. The problem from your point of view is that it is such a low probability activity.

When companies place ads in the newspapers, they often get huge responses. This is especially true in uncertain economic times. It is not uncommon to receive 400, 500, even 1,000 responses to a particular help wanted ad. The person on the receiving end of that paper deluge has a problem. There is no way that hundreds of people are going to be interviewed. At best 5 to 10 people are going to be called in for an interview. So there sits your answer to the ad in the pile of hundreds of others. The odds of you getting a call are very low. And it has nothing to do with you. It is mostly out of your control. So when people tell me that they sent out hundreds of copies of their resume in answer to ads and they never got any response, I'm not surprised. Nor, at this point, should you be. It simply is a very low probability activity for the job hunter. But should you respond to newspaper ads? Yes, of course, you should. Some people actually get jobs that way. You might be one of them. The point is that you shouldn't base your whole job search campaign on answering help wanted ads in the newspapers.

If you're going to respond to ads, then you should at least do it correctly. A typical ad is quoted below along with a recommended response letter. In the first paragraph of your letter give the date of the ad, the name of the newspaper, and the title of the job that you're applying for. The reason for this is that a company may be running many ads and, if you have little chance of getting a response, you have no chance if your letter gets in the wrong pile. Next the letter spells out point by point how your experience and qualifications match the ones spelled out in the ad. You may feel that a particular requirement is not germane to the job at hand but the fact is that your opinion doesn't count. If you feel that putting these requirements in a table is a little heavy handed and doesn't match your style, then by all means, express the thought in another way. If you make it easy for the person reviewing the resumes and letters to include your letter, then maybe yours will land in the interview pile rather than the trash pile.

Notice that the phone number is included in the letter. There is nothing dumber that an answer to an ad that doesn't prominently display the phone number. But I have seen it. Someone, who otherwise would have been interviewed, wasn't because they didn't include their phone number and the interviewer didn't know how to reach them by phone.

Don't respond with a form letter. This is a negative that could be used to put your letter aside. Remember that the person doing the initial screening is looking for a way to put each and every resume aside. Any negative will do as an excuse in this stage of the process. Does this surprise you? Imagine yourself with 1,200 resumes to review. What would you do? You need to get through the process and find 4-5 reasonable people to be interviewed. Besides if you're in Human Resources doing the screening whoever they hire is not going to work for you. Is that too cynical? Maybe but maybe not!

Always indicate what job you're applying for. Companies sometimes run a number of different ads for a number of different jobs. If you make it difficult for the reviewer to know what job you are applying for you're just asking for your letter to be discarded.

My natural inclination is to say not to try to be cute in your letter to get attention. However, this sometimes works if you hit the right note with the screener. The problem is that you have no way of knowing what the right note is. It's out of your control.

Notice that the request for salary history is not honored. If it turns out that your salary is slightly above what is the salary range for the job being offered, then you won't be interviewed. If you are interviewed, and they decide that they want you, most companies can adjust their salary ranges to match your experience. And the reality is that if the opportunity is right, you'll adjust your salary requirements.

Don't send in your letter right away. Let a few days after the ad appeared go by before you mail your letter. The reason for this is that on the receiving end, you get the major response on the first day and then the number of letters dwindles. When do you think your letter has the best chance of being read; on the day when 600 letters arrive or on the day the 5 letters arrive?

The Newspaper Ad

Let's say that you see an ad that reads: "MANAGER, MANUFACTURING for a small plant in SE. Must have 5-10 yrs. exp. with plastic inj. molding. TQM and MRP exp desired. College deg. required. Send resume and salary history to Box 23456."

Your Answering Letter

Your answer to this might read something like this—

Dear Sir:

This is in response to your ad in last Sunday's *Morning Star Newspaper* for a Manufacturing Manager. The following shows how my experience fits your requirements:

Your Requirements	My Experience
5-10 years Experience as a Manufacturing Manager.	I have 8 years exp.
Injection Molding	I have 13 years exp.
MRP	Helped install MRP APICS certified
TQM	Started quality circles
College degree	BS in Industrial Eng.

As you can see, my experience fits your requirements quite well. Please call me, (215) 555-5555, or email me at myemail@job.com so that we can set up a time for a meeting.

Sincerely yours,

෨෨

Dealing with Recruiters

Some of the ads that you see may be placed by employment recruiters. Recruiters work for companies and are paid by companies. They either are paid on a contingency basis (i.e, they get paid if you take the job) or they are being paid to do a search. Generally, they do not keep resumes on file. They may call companies with your resume in front of them but they are only using it as transparent reason to call. The micro-second the company indicates that they are not interested in you the recruiter is on to the next idea. That does not mean that you shouldn't deal with recruiters. You should because there may be a job available and you might be the one to get it. One of the most interesting jobs I ever got came through a recruiter. However, it's important to remember how the recruiter gets paid and to understand that they don't work for you. Under no circumstances should you pay someone to do a job search for you.

∂∽∽

Internet Searches

The things that are said about answering newspaper ads also apply to the internet. Go ahead and answer ads on the internet. Some people actually get jobs this way. The problem from your point of view again is that it is such a low probability activity. There is a vast array of job search internet sites. Internet sites get paid by having advertisers on the site. Unlike the newspapers most of the advertisers don't pay to display their ads but only pay the site owner if you click on the ad. The site owners may also be selling you services. Their business model is based on driving as many users to their site as possible. One of the ways that they may try to do this is to collect your information and send you an unending stream of email to entice you to come back to the site many times. The more often you visit the site the more likely you are to click-through one of the ads. Remember this is how they get paid. The characteristics of these sites are:

1. They display ads for companies that have jobs.
2. They may have a place for you to post your resume.
3. They may offer advice on many aspects of getting a job.
4. Some sites require you to register (give them your email address) to use the site.
5. If you want to answer one of the ads, you will most likely have to register to do so.
6. Some will offer to help you write your resume for a fee. There is no good reason to do this. It's a waste of your

money that will not produce any results for you.

7. Some will offer to send your resume to companies for a fee. This is sometimes called broadcasting your resume. There is no good reason to do this. It's a waste of your money that will not produce any results for you.

8. Some will charge you to post your resume. I can't imagine any good reason for paying someone for what you can get for free.

9. Some will have useful search engines to help find the right kind of job.

10. Many of the sites have the same owner so that as you navigate through the site you may find that you are directed to another site.

There are a number of different sites that you might try. The landscape changes almost daily so my advice is to use you favorite search engine to find what's out there. Just remember that this is a low probability activity. Here are a few places to look:

http://www.monster.com/. Notice that there is a place for first timers to go for help. There are directions for doing a job search and for posting your resume and this service is free.

This site is very professional looking with videos and articles.

http://www.careerbuilder.com/. There is a resources and advice section. This site is another very professional looking site with videos and articles. You can post your resume on this site and search the listed jobs.

http://www.job.com. This site is typical of a number of sites on the internet. They want you to register before you can use the site. They want this information so they can send you emails that will get you to go to the website. This is not necessarily a bad thing as long as you understand the process.

http://www.indeed.com. You can't post a resume on this site but it is very easy to navigate through the job postings.

http://www.flipdog.com. This site has a really great search engine that was very easy to use.

http://www.usajobs.opm.gov/. USAJOBS is the Federal Government's official one-stop source for Federal jobs and employment information. Sites like this could be very useful if you're are looking for a government job. There will likely be a similar website for your state or for a large municipality.

http://www.snagajob.com. I found this website very interesting. They bill themselves as "the No. 1 source for hourly employment (and a friend to the hourly worker)".

http://www.pinkslipmixers.com. I heard about this site listening to Fox News. It's run by people looking for work and trying to help each other. Check it out.

These are but a few of the websites you might look at. If you belong to a professional society you may find that they have a job posting section on their website. Just don't make this your main activity. It should be a sideline activity.

Finally, don't forget to check http://www. MyEasyJobSearch.com. This site is being updated regularly with new material. This is a really great site that contains all the material that we didn't think of when we were writing this book.

✌✌

How the People You Deal with Get Paid

The expression is, "Follow the money." When you understand how the people that you will come in contact with and deal with during your job search get paid, then you'll better understand your relationship to them.

Newspapers

This is how newspapers get paid. First of all you bought the paper. The advertisers paid to have their ads in the paper. The employers paid to have their ad in the paper. Generally, the newspaper is not interested in collecting your personal information.

Internet Sites

Internet sites get paid by having advertisements on the site. Unlike the newspapers, most of the advertisers don't pay to display their ads but only pay the site owner if you click on the ad. The site owners may also be selling you services. Their business model is based on driving as many users to their site as possible. One of the ways that they may try to do this is to collect your information and send you email to entice you to come back to the site many times. The more often you visit the site the more likely you are to click-through one of the ads. Remember this is how they get paid.

Recruiters

Recruiters are generally paid by the companies in one of two ways. Companies sometimes pay a recruiter to do a search. A more usual arrangement is that recruiters get paid a fee if you take a job. No matter how it seems, they do not work for you. They are not going to find you a job. That's your job. Nobody "owes" you a job. Remember, there is a lot of competition out there!

Staffing Firms

Staffing firms hire you and send you on an assignment to companies that then pay them a fee over and above the wage that you are paid. They may also be paid a fee if you are hired permanently by the company that you are assigned to. Staffing firms offer a wide variety of services including temporary work, temp-to-hire work, direct-hire placements, human resource outsourcing, recruitment process outsourcing, *etc.*

Book Authors

In the spirit of full disclosure we offer the following. The authors get paid a royalty when you buy the book. If you borrowed this copy from a friend, we urge you to go out and buy your own copy. Notice that we also have a website.

ॐॐ

Your Resume

You will notice, I hope, that I have left the subject of a resume for last. You might think

that I've done this because I think that this subject is unimportant. If you think that, then you'd
be right. Nobody ever got a job because of a
great resume.

The main purpose of a resume should be
something to leave behind after an interview
to remind the potential employer of your value.
It's an advertising piece to attach to a follow-
up letter.

Fill your resume with your accomplishments. You should have a list of these from your
work earlier when you were deciding what you
wanted to do.

Some simple rules that you should follow:

1.   Never include a picture unless you're
      applying for a modeling job.
2.   Use white paper unless you're apply-
      ing for a job as an interior decorator
      or an artist.
3.   I have said for a number of years that
      resumes do NOT have to be printed.
      That a clean copy will do just as well.
      However, with the advent of word-
      processing and laser printers, a pro-
      fessional looking print job is within the
      reach of everybody.
4.   Neatness counts.

5. Don't include references and don't even bother to say that you'll give references. Of course, you'll give references. Who wouldn't?

6. Neatness counts. And so does spelling. (We know that we repeated "Neatness counts." It bears repeating.)

7. Only two pages. It is questionable whether even the first page gets read. More than two pages most definitely will not be even looked at. If you have trouble getting your resume down to two pages, start leaving things out. Leave out those earlier uninteresting things that you did before you got to the interesting stuff. I saw a resume recently of a man who was a dentist. He started his experience with a job he'd had as a waiter! Seriously! Leave out the stuff that nobody cares about! However, you do it, only two pages. No exceptions. Only two pages! Having said all that, many today are advising only one page. This may not be a bad idea. It's not likely that any more than one page will actually be read.

8. Don't include anything else. No letters of reference. No college transcripts. No certificates from conferences. No

copies of your college degree. No one is even going to glance at any resume that includes dozens of pages. Truly, I have seen this. But I didn't read the resume nor will anyone else. If you have to send out copies of your college degree, send a copy to your mother, she'll be proud of you. Don't include it with your resume.

9. Do include at least a one-inch margin on all sides. This will increase the likelihood that your resume will be read. When someone looks at a resume that completely fills the page, and it's the three hundredth resume that they've look at that day, trust me on this, it's not going to be looked at. It's going in the trash pile.

10. List your experience in reverse chronological order. Forget about functional resumes. I don't know about others, but functional resumes give me a headache.

11. List your objective at the top of the resume. If you have a problem narrowing down your objective, have more that one resume. Another way to handle this problem is to leave the objective out of the resume and put it in a cover letter. With the functionality of the word processor you can

make many different versions of your resume, printing-out a fresh copy for every occasion. Whatever you do, don't answer an ad for a job that's vastly different from your objective as listed on the resume. For example, don't answer an ad for a sales job, with a resume that shows your objective as manufacturing management. Do you think that sounds far fetched? What does that kind of action say about the person answering the ad? What pile does the resume go in? Trash, you say? You got it!

12. Except for the two-page rule maximum, none of these rules are hard and fast. It's your job campaign. If you feel more comfortable doing things a little differently, then by all means do so. However, keep reviewing the responses that you're getting. If people giggle when you hand them your resume, perhaps you need to rethink your decision to print your resume in white ink on brown paper.

ॐॐ

Evaluating a Job Offer

The whole purpose of a job search is to get job offers. When you do get them you'll have to decide if you want to accept the job. Usually, a job offer involves what you currently earn in compensation and what assets you bring to the table. In a time of high demand for your specific trade or discipline, you maybe able to negotiate a better deal, however, you need to be aware of certain variables.

When considering an offer you should not only look at the salary amount being offered but the total package.

Some employers offer a high salary but fall short when it comes to their benefit packages. Other employers offer packages that include strong medical coverage, lucrative time off with pay, benefits, life insurance, stock options, *etc*. In cases like these the salary offer from an employer with the strong benefit package may not seem as attractive as another employer's, however it is important that you make a fair apples-to-apples comparison of the overall package. Lastly, in comparing offers you will need to know what your out of pocket expenses will be for the different medical plans and what they cover. It is also relevant to find out what percentage of the medical insurance premium the employer pays. As an example; if one employer pays 50% of your medical insurance premium and another only pays 30%, an offer of 50 cents an hour given to you from this second potential employer may not be the best offer.

Employers generally have to take into consideration several variables when making salary offers to external candidates. Some of these variables include what other employers pay (the market average) for those within the same trade or discipline, existing incumbent's salaries, the amount of experience/education the new candidate possesses and their salary history. Generally employers will share with applicants what the minimum, mid and maximum rates are for the position available.

As mentioned before, if you work in an industry where your expertise is in high demand, you come highly recommended, and/or have a well known reputation in your industry; you should fare well through the negotiation process. You could also do well if your expertise could potentially save the employer a great deal of money by not having to outsource.

For the rest of us, generally a prospective employer will take into account your experience, salary history along with your realistic salary expectations when formulating your salary offer. The reason the term realistic is used is because we all think we are worth more then what we are paid but let's be fair minded. If you are job hunting and currently earning $50,000 dollars a year, chances are you are going to receive an offer around that same amount, even though you would like to be paid $70,000. This of course would be different if the company minimum for the position you have applied for is more then what you are currently earning. Remember, for reasons which include compliance with Wage and Hour Regulations as well as equity to existing employees, an offer will have already taken into account your experience/education and compared that to existing incumbents to best place you, from a compensation standpoint, where you fit within their ranks. While you may have a small window of negotiating room on your salary offer, companies will feel they are limited in their ability to respond to your desires. One of their top priorities will be to not unset existing salary structures as well as respecting existing employee loyalty.

ॐॐ

After You Get a Job

Remember that "A Scout is courteous." And perhaps you remember your mother telling you to always write "bread and butter letters." You don't? Perhaps that is the generation gap. My mother always told me to write a thank you letter after a visit. The idea was to thank my host for their hospitality. This thank you note was called a "bread and butter" note. Be sure to write a "bread and butter" letter to every one that helped you during your job search. Simply say that you're writing to thank them for help-ing you when you were looking for a job. Tell them about the new job. After all you'll need to call on them again for the next job search. Perish the thought.

Chapter 6
Other Things That You May Want to Know

This section will include some other things that you may find helpful.

Doing a Professional Job of Getting Fired

If you're going to get fired, then you might as well do it professionally. Remember that lay-off and firing are stress situations both for you and for the person firing you.

One of the most stressful interviews that you'll ever have is the one where you're being fired or laid-off. Nothing will be gained by losing your cool at this juncture. Remember that as stressful as it might be for you it may be just as unnerving for the person whose sad duty it is to do the firing or laying-off. I remember one such occasion when I had been fired (or laid-off, if you prefer) more often than the manager that was firing me had never fired someone. I suspect it was the first time for him. This is the time when you may have some bargaining power. Ask for a bigger severance pay. Ask for outplacement services. Ask to be able to keep your company email address. Ask for a reference letter. Ask for a copy of your personnel file. Ask for anything that you can think of that might help you get your next job. After all, the worst they can say is, "No." They just might say, "Yes."

Above all, do not get angry. Do not burn any bridges. They may discover in a few weeks that they have made a terrible mistake in letting you go and will want to bring you back. Maybe they'll want to hire you as a consultant to straighten out the mess that your successor made. (Just remember consultants get much more than you were making. Don't go back for your old rate.) Make notes about what is being said to you. Don't sign any termination contracts until your lawyer has seen them.

After you get home it's OK to get mad and throw things. This is natural. Express your anger. Get over it. Move on. Don't dwell on how unfair the world is. The world is unfair. Get over it. Move on.

෯෯

Sign Up For Unemployment Compensation.

Sign up for unemployment compensation. Do it right away. There usually is a waiting period so the sooner you sign up the sooner you can start collecting. I know that your cousin told you you're not eligible because you were born out of state or something but it's not his call. If you're not eligible, let the bureaucrats tell you. And if they do, appeal it. Remember that unemployment compensation is taxable income even though you don't have to have taxes withheld. At the same time job hunting expenses may be deductible if you itemize deductions. (And don't take tax advice from guys writing a job search book. Get professional help in this area too.)

❧❧

Budget

Go over you budget and see how your finances are going to be in the months ahead. It could take many months to get your next situation. Cut you expenses where you can. This is not a good time to go on a spending spree. You may get immediate gratification but in the long run you suffer if you can't make the payments or if you've used cash that you later need. It's amazing how far you can cut your expenses. Unless you live a very frugal life you can do an amazing job of cutting back. Even if you get unemployment compensation it will likely be much less than you were making.

৵৵

Job Loss Support

Make contact if you can with job loss support groups in your area. Tell all your friends and relatives that you're out of work and looking for a new situation. This is not a secret that needs to be kept. There is no shame in being out of work. Whatever you do, don't keep this a secret from your spouse and family. You'll need their support to get through this situation.

৵৵

Know Your Rights

Whether you are involved in a mass layoff or you're the only one that has been asked to leave, you do have rights.

In order to try and avoid post employment litigation, those who are protected by law (a minority race, women, those 40 or older, and those with disabilities) or have established a good deal of seniority with an employer may be offered a package upon their release, even in some cases where the employee is accused of misconduct. As mentioned above, the window of time that is usually afforded should be spent reviewing the terms and conditions with your legal counsel. Failure to do so may result in your signing some of your rights away. Sometimes these terms and conditions can be further negotiated, however only do so after reviewing your options and negotiation strategies with your legal counsel

Most larger employers offer some kind of dispute or grievance review program. If you believe the action being taken adversely affects you, these can be good forums where individual circumstances (such as back pay, perceived disparate treatment, etc.) can be taken into account and further discussed.

Always seek out employment law legal counsel before making any employment decisions especially before signing anything. Here too is a good opportunity to remind you, do not take legal advice from guys writing a job search book, or for that matter others who believe they are lawyers.

༺༻

Fair Employment

Companies that have contracts with the federal government equaling $10,000.00 dollars or more a year are an Affirmative Action Employer. Generally you will be able to determine whether or not you have applied at an Affirmative Action Employer by the signage displayed in their employment lobby or ad copy in their wanted ads. Affirmative Action Employers can be held accountable if their employee base does not closely reflect the population demographics of the area in which they conduct business.

❧❧

Employment Discrimination

Most employers are obligated by law to recruit and fill job openings in a non-discriminatory fashion. There are certain questions that an employer cannot ask you during an interview and, if they do, they may have violated the law. Companies cannot ask you about (unless you bring the subject up first):

- Your age
- Your ethnicity
- The religion you practice

- Your marital status or questions about your family
- If you have a disability, health or medical problems
- How you plan on getting to work

If you are asked questions along this nature and/or you feel you did not get the position due to unfair selection practices, the first recommended step is to contact the individual who is in charge of the company's Human Resources Department, or for larger companies the individual who is in charge of Employment. Generally, by doing so, an additional interview is scheduled and conducted by a more senior member of the Human Resources Team to ensure fairness. If you are not given this opportunity or you still feel the selection process was unfair you can either move on or contact your area's Equal Employment Agency or a similar government agency.

ॐ∞

Extra Reading

Early drafts of this book listed additional books about looking for work. However, we now think this seems silly. We have written, and you have now read, the definitive book on job searching so why should you need any additional reading material.

That being said, there are a few books that we think are important and that you should read so that you have a better understanding of the world today—the world where you are trying to find gainful employment. These are:

Thomas Friedman, *The World is Flat*, Farrar, Straus and Giroux, 2005

William Bridges, *Jobshift—How to Prosper in a Workplace Without Jobs,* Da Capo Press, 1995

Eliyahu M. Goldratt, *The Goal*, 3rd edition, North River Press, 2004

Aubrey Daniels, *Bringing Out the Best in People*, 2nd edition, McGraw-Hill, 1999

Steven Levitt and Stephen J. Dubne, *Freakonomics: A Rogue Economist Explores the Hidden Side of Everything,* William Morrow, 2005

Malcolm Gladwell, *The Tipping Point: How Little Things Can Make a Big Difference,* Little Brown , 2000

৵৶

Acknowledgements

First of all we wish to thank the hundreds of folks that have given us job interviews over the years. Your help is really appreciated. Then we need to thank those that we have interviewed. Your patience with us as we learned the process is commendable. We would especially like to thank those who, after being given a draft of this book in the hopes that it would help with their job search, were kind enough to offer feedback.

Specifically we'd like to thank David Prine for helping with the editing and Kristi Gage-Linderman of Gage Personnel Employment Services for some very helpful suggestions. Our friend of many years, Robert Jones, has often given us great advice which we found useful. Finally, we thank Ernie Daley who was kind enough to do the final edit.